THE SORROW APARTMENTS

Also by Andrea Cohen

The Cartographer's Vacation
Long Division
Kentucky Derby
Furs Not Mine
Unfathoming
Nightshade
Everything

THE SORROW APARTMENTS

ANDREA COHEN

Four Way Books
Tribeca

for you

Library of Congress Cataloging-in-Publication Data

Names: Cohen, Andrea, 1961- author.
Title: The sorrow apartments / Andrea Cohen.
Identifiers: LCCN 2023031704 (print) | LCCN 2023031705 (ebook) | ISBN
9781954245785 (trade paperback) | ISBN 9781954245792 (ebook)
Subjects: LCGFT: Poetry.
Classification: LCC PS3603.O3415 S67 2024 (print) | LCC PS3603.O3415
(ebook) | DDC 811/.6--dc23/eng/20230731
LC record available at https://lccn.loc.gov/2023031704
LC ebook record available at https://lccn.loc.gov/2023031705

This book is manufactured in the United States of America and printed on
acid-free paper.

Four Way Books is a not-for-profit literary press. We are grateful for the
assistance we receive from individual donors, public arts agencies, and private
foundations including the NEA, and the New York State Council on the Arts, a
state agency.

PROUD MEMBER

[c|mp]

We are a proud member of the Community of Literary Magazines and Presses.

Contents

And I remember the whole of that day vividly, though nothing particular happened.

—Anton Chekhov

REMEMBER

The mind's the finest
gardener—in deepest

snows, the plum
tree blossoms.

I

UFOS

I believe that things
fly, that I don't know
what they are or what
they might signify.
I see them all
the time, behind
the drive-in, inside
my friend's eyelids,
and just as frequently
I witness objects
I can't identify except
to say they seem
like children about
to ask a question.
Does everyone get
their own sky? Is life
really like a bullet
you try to ride, or
more like a buffet
of baffling appetizers
and entrées? Is it all
you can steal? I
steel myself
to the mysteries, to

believing everything flies
in the face of classification.
Why else would Miss Hestle
have gathered us that afternoon
in a glassy room in third grade
to watch her cry? Outside,
monarch butterflies were
auditioning for a movie
called *The World is Full
of Mystery and Wonder*
and we hovered above
our futures, we beat
our wings in
ways we have
failed, in essay
after essay, ever
to replicate.

ADJACENT

My life was going on
in the next room. There

were board games and
Pinochle, there were people

talking over each other. They
were making borscht, they

were making flowers out of pink
and blue tissue. Whatever you do, don't

cry into them, someone was
bawling. I was in the room

with the adjoining door,
listening, the way a child

warm and dry might
listen to rain.

MATERIALS & METHODS

That it was
a ceramic

animal isn't
material. It

was a fawn.
It lived

under an awning.
You can choose

loneliness
or courage.

I gave it
all my porridge.

DINOSAURS IN MY HEAD

How
did they get there?

They
heard the word

extinction—
and being wise

creatures
decided to hide

where
fire and ice,

where
time couldn't find them.

MAGNET

What Ray Finney did
at Savannah Steel I
never knew. He gave
me magnets stamped
with the company name—
emerald shafts the color
of money but better
than cash: they had
heft and picked things
up: gem clips, fountain
pens, costume jewelry. You
had to be careful where you
left them, my mother said:
a magnet could make a wrist-
watch stop. It was a trick, I
thought, like giving a child
a cherry from a sweet
Rob Roy. Nobody had told
me yet that days are all
temporary, and the afternoon
Ray Finney wasn't playing
dead in our backyard, I
held a magnet above him,
someone said, like a magic

wand or blunt instrument. I
never knew what he was
doing in our house, why
my mother pulled the drapes
tight, mid-day, what happened
to time, how I could not fix it.

FOX

I saw my first movie
downtown at The Fox. It
was a double feature—
The Future playing
on the same screen
as *The Past*, and
beneath the ninety-six
stars of the Arabian sky,
I spilled my Coke and
someone scolded me
and someone cleaned me up,
and a sad usher in a bowtie
and flashlight cried quietly
as the summer matinée
of rain played on
the minarets and turrets
of that architectural mash-
up of Alhambra and Karnak,
and down the street, there
were cannons and Confederate
flags outside Johnny Reb's,
and people who believed
in progress picketed while
men in Civil War uniforms

distributed leaflets that said
Everyone loves Johnny Reb's
ice cream. You can love
the ice cream and hate
the hand that makes it.
You can see it all
in a silent news clip
in black and white.
You can see *The Past*
and *The Future* on two reels,
and what were moving
pictures back then anyway,
but a series of stills
strung together, spilling
out under a trompe l'oeil
night—just another
highly flammable
illusion of motion.

FLIGHT PATTERN

I was five when I found
the head of the wren

by the road. I was older
when I found its wing.

By then, it was impossible
to piece even the idea

of a bird back together.

FREIGHT

What weighs
more—

pound
of feathers

or the memory
of thinking

you
might fly?

RAIN, 1966

Dark, out
and in.

Tomorrow—
cake, but

today, someone
is watering

the lake.

MERCURIAL

We were bored
to tears, breaking

thermometers open,
letting the silver

drops spill and scatter and
reassemble in our hands.

We didn't understand
how dangerous that was—

our hands, I mean, meaning
to hold anything.

LUCKY STRIKES

We smoked them so we
could blow smoke rings—

little halos above
coffee cups, above dish

rags and coupons
our mothers clipped

back when the earth
employed them.

SPRINKLER

The children
    were running

through it—
    you could see

how rivers
    could envy

        a spigot.

AWAKENING

I found my mother
asleep, midday, slung

across the foot of the bed
in her blue dress. It

frightened me—how
log-like she seemed,

she who had always
been a tree.

PIÑATA

It's not a lot
to blindfold
a child, to
give him
a couple good
spins and
a wooden
bat, to tell
him to swing
his little
heart out.
Harder is
to stock
the piñata
with rotted
plums, with
nettles, with
a confetti
of IOUs—
to fill that
hollowness
with
consequences,
with the truth

about how
nothing swung
at blindly—
with force
and glee—
yields anything
resembling sweets.

BACK TO SCHOOL.

Mostly this includes
glue—glue and paste,

paste and tape. By
extension, we conclude

that autumn is a kind
of triage for everything

summer was—the
bursting open, the coming

apart, as when, at
dusk, at the cul-de-sac,

someone throws a ball
up and everyone

runs. Wondering what
the point of that game

was is like asking
the purpose of summer,

of evenings when
one mother calling

called us all in.

LAMAR T.

He was a pallbearer
at my mother's

wedding, I said,
and once I'd

said it, I knew
it was wrong

to speak so
openly of

private matters.

SOMETHING

Something went wrong.
That's what the machine
says when I call to say
my paper didn't arrive.
Machines are trained
by people, so they're
smart, they know a thing
or fifty trillion. Did you miss
your Sunday delivery?
it asks. I did, I say. I
miss everything, I say,
because it's a machine and
it has to listen, or at least
it has to not hang up
without trying to understand
why I called, which means
trying to correct what
went wrong. Let me
see if I got this right,
the voice says, you missed
your Sunday paper?
Yes, I say, but also
I miss my childhood
and fairy tales,

like Eden. I miss
sweet Rob Roys
with strangers,
I miss fabric
softener and soft
lighting. I'm sorry,
the machine says. I'm
having trouble understanding.
Did you miss today's paper?
Yes, I say, but that's not
the half of it. Sometimes
I just feel like half
of me, and even that
feels like too much. I'm
having trouble understanding,
the machine repeats, its
syllables halted, as if
trying to mimic an empath.
I'm having trouble understanding
too, I say. I used to understand
so much: photosynthesis, the
human heart, I'd even
memorized the Krebs cycle,
but now all I remember

is lifting the golden coil
of the kitchen phone to maneuver
under my mother's conversations.
It was like lifting
the horizon. There's
a silence, and the machine
asks: Are you still there? In
a few words, please describe
your issue. Where do I begin
being a minimalist? Time,
I say, I've got a problem
with that. Also, loss, and
attachment. That's pretty
much it, and the news in its sky-
blue sleeve is meant to be
a distraction, isn't it? I ask.
More silence, and then:
You miss your mother?
a voice asks. It's
a human voice.
Me too, she says.

II

PURCHASE

John Bronzina, I
think you could save me.
You have green eyes
and have completed
your training for CPR
for children and adults.
John, I am in the latter
category, and though
my breathing is fine
now, things change rapidly.
You know this because you
have a card for emergency
roadside service. John,
it is expired. You
have a dental appointment
in six days. Don't
miss it. You have
credit cards and debit
cards and what you do
at The Lemming Emporium
is your business. But I
wonder: What were you doing
when you lost that wallet?
When I found it, I'd stopped

my car on Ocean View to look
at a house being built on stilts.
It's behind a fence that says
KEEP OUT. Nearby there's a pile
of beer cans and I wonder
if you had something
to do with that. Maybe
you sat back under the scrub
pines getting drunk with friends
or on your own. Maybe you
were imagining you lived there,
that you'd gotten locked out and
were waiting for your wife
or your boyfriend
or both of them to let you in.
That's what life is, John—people
opening. You know this, you
live in Connecticut. You know
the president and CEO
of The Invisible Bridge Corporation.
His card is in your wallet. Maybe
you applied for a job there. Maybe
you got it. I had a job once
at Tollbooths of America, but

they let me go. Or more accurately,
I preferred the short-term pain
of leaving to the long-term injury
of staying in one place. What
are your goals, John Bronzina?
Do you think about how you'll feel
when you get where you're
headed? I never think about a place
until I've left it. Things
take time, John. You'll come
to understand that. You have
a birthday coming up. You'll
be twenty-five. On your
driver's license, you're trying
to smile. You're an organ
donor. Parts of you may
one day spill into others,
the way your wallet
tumbled from you, the
way your cards and badges
and cash flew into the bazaar
of salt air and sea grasses
where there's nothing
to buy or sell, just another

trespasser in soft sand
struggling for what we
sometimes—where I
come from—call purchase.

ACAPULCO

He was talking about the random
axe of God, his hand slamming
the table like a battle axe, and though
I was a non-believer, I believed
(I knew) we were sitting, against all odds,
together, with nothing but a checkered
tablecloth between us, in North Bay, where
the maître-d embraced him and seemed to
want to hug me too. The man had written
to say he'd known my father would die
one day, that he'd been preparing nearly
forty years for that, since he was seventeen,
and had needed a psychiatrist roughly
his father's age, Jewish, and on the right
bus line. By then, he said, his father had
been dead five years. My father, he said,
was the first person he confessed his love
of men in dark suits to. *How gentle, he was,*
the man said. *How wise. He was the father*
I didn't have, the man said, and I thought, he
was the father I didn't have either.
The man was a public defender,
and when the waiter brought the wrong
cut of beef, he said, *Everyone is innocent*

of something. We were sitting like
two people who had met in another
life and were trying to catch up. I asked
what had happened to his father and he
said *swimming* and *Acapulco*. He said
shark. And it occurred to me that we
were breaking breadsticks together because
a fish had mistaken a man for something
else. It's a big, random axe. "It Never Entered
My Mind" was playing above and around us—
a sea of Sinatra. *That was your father's favorite,*
the man said, which surprised me, because
I always thought my father liked music
unburdened by words, the way he liked his
evenings with us. I didn't tell the man
about the app you can get now, how it tells
you where sharks are in real time. I didn't
tell him about the woman who reaches
into the mouths of hammerheads to cut
hooks out, how after she's pulled a hook
from one shark, others approach, sensing,
no, *knowing*, she means to help them.
That's a belief system. The world is teeming
with them, and leaving the restaurant,

the man pointed out, as men tend to,
the stars comprising Orion's Belt—
as if it were the lustrous sparks and not
the leveling dark that connects us.

VOLUNTEERS

A cavalry
of flowers
rides in—

THE SORROW APARTMENTS

Who would name a place
that and why am I
standing in front of them?
A man in a gray
face and matching
jacket asks: Are you
Andrea? And I am
surprised and say, I am.
He reaches into his pocket. I
have keys for you, he says,
gesturing at the brutalist
structure, and I'm confused,
having only gone out
for a short walk and by
chance found myself
here. Oh no, I tell him, you
want some other Andrea—
one an X-ray glimpsed
a troubling shadow in,
one whose parachute was
too casually packed. That's
the Andrea you're after, I say,
but he seems unconvinced.

Andrea Cohen? he asks.
Yes, I admit, but there
are so many of us: a rabbi
and a rabbi's wife, a porn
star, a murderer. We're
a dime a dozen, I tell him.
He nods and sighs, he sits
down on a tired bench. I'm
tired too and sit beside him.
Do you have kids? he asks.
No, I say. Me neither, he replies.
Do you want to see them?
He opens his wallet. They're
with my ex, he says, producing
snapshots of a girl and boy
whose faces have been
erased by how many times
his thumb has touched them.
The children are standing
in front of a fountain. It's
dusk in the pictures and
in the world and we compare
wishing wells we wish we could

get back to. He can't remember
when he began his life as the door-
man and Mr. Fixit at The Sorrow
Apartments. I can't remember
when I first learned that people
who are lost tend to wander
in ever-tightening circles.
It's one of those nights
of talking into the dark
until the sun
interrupts you. By
then, I notice that the sign
for *The Sorrow Apartments*
is gone, replaced by one
that reads: *The Wonder Estates,*
Under New Management.
That's strange, I say.
Not really, he says, there
are so many signs, they're
always changing: *Happy*
Acre, Wistful Cottages,
Paradise Place. In another
life, I might have said

that he and I had met
in another life. I take
the keys. Sorrow
is complicated.

CAUSE AND EFFECT

I lost my
way—why

did I ever
think it mine?

RHUBARB AND GARBAGE

We're auditioning for a movie
called *The World is a Mystery,
Isn't It?* We're hoping to be
extras in what's rumored to be
a period piece—though we don't
know which period. Eras are
messy. They don't end
with punctuation. Ice melts
over time, and we find ourselves
in the Stone Age, we find that
the Romans have taken over.
Over near the port-o-johns,
someone says this is meant
to be an epic, someone says
that those chosen will be paid
in pine cones or in three
ages hence. We hear that
the movie is set on the French
Riviera, or during the French
Revolution, which would explain
those guillotines near the craft table.
Also rumored: This is a sequel
to the last silent Spaghetti Western
set in space, and because I'm

a method actor, I begin orbiting
quietly around the parking lot,
where lots of extra-wannabees
are camped out in lawn chairs.
There's chatter that those
who can speak Esperanto
without an accent will go
to the front of the line, that
preference will be given to those
who don't complain about
costumes last laundered in
the Ming Dynasty. I've heard
there's a mob scene (there's
always a mob scene) and that
some of us will be asked to sing
Three Blind Mice while others
scream *rhubarb and garbage,*
a phrase which, for some reason,
when shouted by enough people
sounds uncannily like a mob
out for blood. I don't mind
telling you: I'm tired. I'm
afraid I may have left
the stove on, I may have left

the fire on in the cave. Did I leave
the baby on the bus? Being
human means having to
remember so much. It
means having to exist
in time, which doesn't
really exist—at least not
in the manner of timelines
made popular in *Encyclopedia
Britannicas*. Remember those?
Time, friends, is an unruly
boss. *Rhubarb and garbage,
rhubarb and garbage.* The Dark
Ages never really went away,
they just got sent to their room
to think about what they'd
done. They think they'd like
to do it all over again, they
think they'll be back, with
the stone and the ice, with
those brutally beautiful
boys with Greco-Roman
tresses, wrestling. Friends, I'm

fed up with practicing being
a creature who stared at the moons
of 2020. I'm thinking I should
go back to my igloo when
the director with his megaphone
yells: *Cut, fantastic, it's a wrap!*
And in my best Esperanto I
yell: *No, no, Mr. DeMille—*
but already the stagehands
are hauling ice in, and pterodactyls,
a Catherine Wheel, a new device
for enjoying tea and biscuits
with the dead. There's a new
director, and she makes a beeline
for me with a small monologue:
You starred in that movie,
The Mystery of the World, Part
80 *(give or take)* Billion. *I loved
the bit where your character
thought she was an extra and
not the goddamned star.*
Gobsmacked, I am. *That
was the whole movie,* I tell her.

Yes, she says. *Brilliant!* she says.
She looks so familiar and so kind
of sad. *Have some tea, she*
says, *have a biscuit.*

MANTLE

I have—
on my mantle—

a jam jar filled
with nails. Every-

thing I love has
burned down,

but I still have
my mantle

and my nail
aquarium. I

still have
my fire.

THE TRUTH COMES OUT

I have always wanted
to be an equation.
Ok, so mostly I've wanted
to wear an equal sign
in my hair or on my
person. What a strange
phrase: *on my person*,
as if my person were
an entity trotting
beside me. I have always
wanted such an entity,
a kind of kind stand-in,
doppelganger, what have
you. So that when I needed
spare bits or a pat on what
I had, or just someone else
to ask the waitress for another
helping of forever, well, *voilà*.
Also, it would be swell
if this back-up me could
speak French pleasingly.
S'il vous plaît? Por favor?
Saying please in any
language can be handy.

Could you loosen the duct
tape of night, *bitte,*
tack, pi fauri? Could
you please tell me
I'm doing the human
thing right? And
while we're at it, that
all things being equal
stuff, I'd like, please,
with a reliable
climbing partner,
to finally get
to the bottom of that.

SPRINGFIELD

Get a room, the dude in the blue Camaro yells.
He's made of rage and tinted glass, and we're
made of desire and what if and what I want
to say is, Dude, we have a room, but we
got hungry. Every three days we have to eat
or get mimosas or get yelled at by you. Get
a room, he yells again, maybe because he thinks
we're hard of hearing, or because it pains
him to see our affection. Maybe he thinks:
what a waste—two women who could have
loved him instead. Instead, we get sandwiches to
go and go back to the room we call our room, which
could be in any motel near any off-ramp in any
Springfield, with its anonymous white walls and towels,
with the empty drawers you love, and the flat-screen
TV that seems to keep getting bigger and flatter.
And since we're taking inventory, let's don't
forget the bedside Bible and the red pen
tucked inside, as if we might be inspired to
make corrections. And come to think of it, I would
like to make some changes in how things turn
out, how they turn on a dime, or over time
crumble. Instead, I listen to you read aloud
from the pamphlets you found in the lobby.

Fun fact: basketball was invented in Springfield, Mass.,
as was vulcanized rubber. The man who wrote
The Cat in the Hat was born here, and perhaps
most importantly, this is the birthplace
of interchangeable parts—or at least where
they first caught on. Think assembly
lines, think mass production. I'm thinking
about the fun fact of you, about how
much I love origin myths, about how people
aren't things. We can't be vulcanized, we
can't, like faulty chains, be replaced. And
I'm thinking about that guy in the Camaro,
how what really drives him is loneliness,
how we see iterations of him in all
the Springfields we find ourselves in,
because that's your fantasy: you and me
in every Springfield in America, in Nebraska
and Ohio and North Dakota, in townships
in Jersey and Michigan, always in a motel
bar, pretending we've never met. And
after a while, after Idaho and Maine,
after Springfields in Kentucky and East
Texas, the myth rings true: it's old hat, old
cat in the hat: the white walls and small

bars of soap, the falling asleep in the middle
of a life, the waking to one place named
for another—not a fun fact exactly,
just what the Russian novelist not
immune to Springfields knew
about unhappiness.

LIFE

It was a hand-
me-down lamb
I got, with lambs-
wool and slobber—
the opposite of
an actual lamb
in that it didn't
bleat or go
to slaughter,
but it could
still, like me,
who left it
on the bus
once, be
a lost sheep—
which are a
dime a dozen,
my older brother,
trying to cheer
me up said.
After our mother
had handed that
lamb from him
to me, he began

carrying a lamp
everywhere. A
damn lamp.
I had to, he
told me later,
on account of being
my brother and bigger,
on account of needing
to get a good look
at everything I'd
love and want
to remember.

ISLAND

Someone said
the wild horses

swam here
and couldn't

swim back—
but it must have

been their own
wildness they

were swimming after.

EAVESDROPPING ON ADAM AND EVE

It didn't get interesting
until after they'd left.
An extended vacation,
Adam called it. *R&*
D, Eve said. *Whatever.*
In Eden, they never
said so much as
pass the salt on
account of everything
tasting so great there.
They were strangers
until they left, when
Adam confessed, *I*
felt penned in there,
and Eve, forgetting how
naked they'd been,
said, *I was always*
waiting for the other
shoe to drop. Now
they're both cobblers,
now they have so much
to talk about: whether
to spring for heat
or vaccines, whether

to call their interiors
climate or weather,
when the next ice age
might hit. Adam pours
himself another
hieroglyph and asks:
What does it all mean?
and Eve does what
she always does:
wraps herself, boa-
like, around him and holds
the camera an arm's
length above for a
this is us moment
for the snake they
miss so much.

CLEAR AND PRESENT

How dangerous
is the snake

oil salesman?
Ask the snake.

AT THE MEMORIAL SERVICE

for Scott Harney

I wanted to steal something
from the bathroom
at the cathedral—
a basinet or plastic hand
towel dispenser—anything
that wasn't nailed down,
though, in the sanctuary, I
was eyeing those things too:
the pews and oak podium,
the organ pipes and bright
eyes in the faces of stained
glass saints. I contemplated
taking the hammered-
down hands and feet
of Jesus in a painting
that was faded and sad
and anatomically incorrect.
Of course, what I wanted
was faith—faith in
the mysteries, faith
in some life after
this one, faith that we might
still see him kneeling
up ahead on the cooled

path to Mt. Vesuvius, still
handsomer than Sal Mineo,
pretending to tie his shoe,
making it a double
knot, while we catch up.

REFUSAL TO MOURN

In lieu of
flowers, send
him back.

THE AIR THERE

We walked past ice
skaters, past children falling
on purpose. *They like*
the drama of it, Jane was
saying. She was staying
with friends near the hospital.
If the trial goes well, she said,
I might move east. It was
an experiment, this trying
to keep her body from dying.
Meanwhile, we headed
west through the park
to an open house, a ground
floor apartment so doll-
like Jane said: *if I die,*
hell better be bigger.
At the coffee shop, she
got a ginger tea. She
apologized to the wall
she bumped into. At 95th Street
she touched the front door
and the elevator button
through her blue scarf—
a precaution. The air

was cold there.
We kissed it.

REGARDING MY DELAY

I've been trying
on coffins

and can't
find one

with a big
enough dance floor.

WAITER

He carries everything
on his tray—
coffee, tea, biscuits.

We sit at a table
the size
of a wheel.

He carries everything
on his tray—
sun, moon, stars.

We nibble biscuits
and the sun. We drink
the moon slowly.

Oh, you who bring us
ourselves, say we
may stay longer.

III

NOTES ON THE TEXT

When I was writing my novel, I was in Sweden,
listening to popcorn not popping. I was thinking

about the burden of plot, how sound drives everything
down the road—or off it. I thought I was listening

to the radio in the Plymouth when Lou Rawls
came on (all bedroom, all let's get it on) and I saw

it was a mix-tape someone had made my wife while I
was buttering day-old toast. You never know what

ditch your road will become, and that there's nothing
new under the sun doesn't mean you don't get burned.

What's with the double negatives? you could ask.
I'm stockpiling them on the off-chance that I might

climb atop them and get a better view, like the one
the realtor from a summer rooftop promised.

Just build up, he said, and you'll get the sea.
He was jumping up when he said this, and did not

not fall. This was in Coralville, Iowa, not far
from the diner where I ordered what sounded like

a Croque Monsieur but ended up being ham on rye,
which the realtor, out of traction, sent back to the kitchen,

explaining that this had been *a failure of the imagination.*
Write that on my headstone, will you? And if there's not

room, write it in the sky, with my ashes—and if
Lou Rawls is there, tell him I miss him.

SWALLOWS

They don't catch
     the light so
        much as

     borrow it,
like a boy
     feinting and leaping

        moon-hit—in
    a pick-up
game of happiness.

CONFLATION

The in-law apartment in Flagstaff was atop
the proper house, on a hill, and when the landlords

boarded their Winnebago, our summer
job was to read P.G. Wodehouse to the figurines,

with feeling. Otherwise, we were forbidden
to hang around the owner's abode, though one

afternoon, fevered, I sought their cooler rooms
out and found, in a darkened den, a chintz throw

on a sofa, and below, a load of Smith & Wessons.
I took riflery in school, and Marriage 101, so

I know what chintz looks like, and what the end
of the road resembles, and seeing those guns I also

saw myself that time I was two-timing in the heart-
land and hid in the cab of a blue pick-up,

under a tartan rug, at the video store, where
my clandestine love was checking out Costa-Gavras'

Missing. Beneath that rug, I discovered what
a bundle of triggers I was, and then we drove

to Lone Tree and called it quits beside a de-
commissioned reconnaissance tank. All

those endings run, lemming-like, together,
every we I knew is commemorated in a paper

weight, but when no one's looking, the papers
slink off. What Chekhov said about the gun

above the mantle is true, but also this:
anything can be a bullet—fever

unchecked, whiff of chintz, that shrapnel
of stars, dizzying, we last saluted.

HISTORICAL REGISTER

This is the house
where we did not.

And this. And this.
The list is very very.

It is what we call extensive.
The register with which

I will lead the tour will
be loud and measured.

I've packed a lunch.
I've hired a bus.

It's just the two
of us—come,

sit closer.

SPINNING THE BOTTLE

It was always
an empty bottle.

We were always
the dark.

Ardor is still
random and dizzy

and someone turns
the lights on

and the room
without the bottle

keeps spinning.

STRETCH

In limbo, I spoke
into the phone,
which transcribed
that as *in limo*.
In limo? she
wrote back.
OMG, she wrote.
She'd asked me
to marry her
habitually, the way
you'd ask someone
to bring home milk.
In limo? she repeated,
this time inside
emojis of station
wagons and champagne,
and I thought, isn't
limbo a kind
of limo—
a stretch
of the actual,
a sawing it
in half and adding
a luxurious bit

to slip into?
What color
is the limo?
she asked.
Glittery, I lied.
Sequined, I added.
At a point one gets
out the saw, one
opens up to
let the mess
and rapture
in. One says,
Home, James!
and the limbo
driver into
elongated
nights drives on.

NIGHTSHIRT

She stepped
out of it

and day
was everywhere.

HOME INVASION

Take me to your leader,
some invaders say—
but these creatures
were different—handsome
and glamorous, some
hairless, some hirsute.
Forsooth, they'd say, apropos
of nothing, bumping into their
idea of us. They had this faraway
doom in their eyes, and a few
not-so-secret rituals involving
absinthe and pistols, and once,
when I was a drive-in bank
teller, one of them, whom
I'll call Mildred, walked
right up to my glass
chest plate and apologized
for not having a car. We're
not actually allowed to drive,
she said. Well, I asked, who
piloted that fancy spaceship?
She shrugged: that stuff
is all automated. I could tell
without her telling me that

this was a stick-up, so I
gave her all my twenties
and fives, because that's
what management teaches
you to do. But she was ruthless,
insisting I hand over all my
best memories. Why
live without those? I
might as well have been
a pocket watch or a gnome,
and I know you're not
supposed to look invaders
in the eye, but I did, which
is how I realized what was
different about these creatures
was the blue of their eyes—
shooter marbles so ghostly
and so incapable of sight.
I couldn't look away, couldn't
not marvel at how ingenious
these creatures were, who
could always claim they'd
never seen themselves do
anything out of the ordinary.

PASSING THE TORCH

It hurts when
they hand it

to you, and
when they

say: pass
it on.

MADRID

Madrid struggles
with record snows,

with roses and rowboats,
with the center of all roads

and even *The Triumph
of Death* snowed in.

Meanwhile, I sit
with my chipped

plate of churros,
with my broken

eggs. Who can
eat? There have

been so many
nos, but this

one fell
from her

lips. It
buries me.

SWAP SHOP

We keep
coming back—

leaving this
mirror for that.

AUBADE

The song she sang
at the breakfast table

she was really singing
for someone else—

but I kept listening.
There was plum jam.

There was toast and sun
coming in—it was like

hearing the notice
of my own death.

SEA SHANTY

When land
is that

abstract,
you have

to sing
your way back.

PASTORAL

You can't swim
in the same

river twice,
but you can

stand at its
edge and

in a thousand
ways recall

her. You
can, over

and over,
go under.

DWELLING

Where do you tell
people you live? she

asked. It depends,
I said, who's asking.

To the man in Tunis,
it's Italy. In Lisbon,

to the barkeep, I'd
say Tuscany, to

the barber in Milan,
Arezzo. To the butcher

down the hill in
Sansepolcro, I'd

say up the hill, in
Castelnuovo, and

to you—well,
I dwell in the room

of questions where
you left me.

SANSEPOLCRO

The room
       of fragments

has been
       restored.

There's
       a chair

there—where
       the guard

lets part
       of me rest.

COTTAGE BLUFF

We board
the summer

windows up—
so they won't

see us leaving.

HORSES

The horses refuse
to go to the moon.

They do not appreciate
Swiss cheese and are

partial to stalls
and barns, where

they're training
a ranch hand,

secretly, not
to break them.

BRIDGE

There was a swinging bridge
above a ravine. It connected

us to fear. It was constructed
of rope and oak and not

looking down. We held on
to the plausibility of falling,

but always reached some
other side. I have a swinging

now inside me, like
buildings engineered

for high winds and quakes —
to sway—and carry on.

IV

SNAKE HANDLER

At last
       I understand

what I was
       afraid of—

looking down
       at my two

hands,
       having nothing

else to be
       afraid of.

STONE AGE

I could—with one
stone—kill two birds,

but then I'd dwell
alone with a blood-

stained stone, one
too morose to build

a stone house with,
and nothing overhead

suggesting a way to fly
outside myself.

EMERGENCY CHOCOLATE CAKE

It's the cake we bake
in wartime, without
eggs or milk, without
flour or chocolate.
We bake it
without ovens or
pans. It's hard
to imagine
sitting around
the bombed-out
kitchen table,
eating it without
hands, without
a mouth, without
saving the recipe
for some knucklehead
in peacetime, in
uniform, gung-
ho to reenact
everything we
went without.

GOD,

I forgive you
for letting
us invent you.

STATE OF THE UNION

Who could
have predicted

such an outcome—
even the fortune

cookie start-
up shuttered.

SWAGGER

We are allowed to watch
snow fall. We are

allowed to catch it
in our virtual mouths.

We are allowed
to remember

springs before this
one, and what it is

to touch and swagger
into summer in the town

square, where eternity
seemed contagious.

PIECEWORK

The piece for fire
and two hands is one

I've been practicing.
I only learned

recently to read
people. One must

develop a taste
for dissonance.

One must
appreciate

that the piece
for fire and two

hands consists
in its entirety

of a scream—
fire beseeching

two hands to
save themselves.

DAFFODILS AND HYACINTHS

Spring has not
been cancelled,

not even
postponed—

ask the daffodils
and hyacinths,

it's only
the clinking

of laughter
that's missing.

JANUARY RAIN

I was waiting for the words
of the song to begin. There
were notes on a piano, a
sitar strummed. There
was a sea and near
the shoreline what
could have been basalt
or charred wood but was,
approach showed, a bird
tucked inside its wing.
I sat down in sand.
Tides spilled in. At
a point, flight
is not an option.
The bird dragged
itself a few feet
dune-ward. I
was waiting
for the words
to begin. Whoever
was crying for
everything cried.

DAPHNE

She can be found
in two places
in the index
in Edith Hamilton's
Mythology: under
Daphne, where
she belongs, and
under *Apollo*,
where she struggled
not to be. There,
it reads: *Apollo,
Daphne loved
by*—as if. As
if overtaking
could be
confused
with love, as
if a woman
didn't have
to choose
between being
Daphne, by
Apollo stolen,
or being—

instead—
a tree be-
yond him.

FIFTEEN TURKEYS

They go everywhere
together. There
used to be
sixteen. I used
to think they
were foraging.
Now I know
they're looking
and listening
for the lumbering
of men, the ones
in camouflage
and orange
vests and caps—
that contradiction
nothing feathered
comprehends.

EPHEMERA

Every pedestal—
a monument
to dust.

CIVIL WAR

I had one son
who played

capture the flag
in the dark—

and another son
who played

another game—
capturing

the dark
in his flag.

FIRING SQUAD

In our line of work,
three men must fire,
because we have three

women to go home to,
three bedstands with lamps,
three shaving mirrors,

and three straight razors
to convince it was
another man's bullet

that hit its mark.

BETWEEN THE WARS

It's the phrase
we had

after the first
war—so don't

say blood-
shed invented

nothing.

BALM

It's a balm,
he said, or

so I thought—
not wanting

bomb to be
the last

word heard.

LIFE & DEATH

They go
hand in hand—

like that little
kid last

seen being
led by

that bigger
kid down

to the river.

BEGINNING (AGAIN)

Small funerals
may resume.

Forgive me
for not

(under
the weight

of this
casket)

clapping.

ELEGY FOR ME

I was what
I loved: lambswool
on the lamb, the glamour
of flesh, memory of
what it is to speak
as evening enters
a room in winter,
snow falling as
in a silent film
called *Us*, and
if a reel breaks,
the genius projectionist
perched above
the darkened theatre
fixes it and begins
again at the beginning.

BUNKER

What would I
think, coming

up after
my world

had evaporated?
I'd wish

I were water.

Acknowledgments

The Adroit Journal: "Something"

The Arkansas International: "The Sorrow Apartments," "UFOs,"
    "Dinosaurs in My Head"

Copper Nickel: "Circular," "Eavesdropping on Adam & Eve,"
    "Civil War"

Diode: "God," "Firing Squad," "Beginning (Again)," "Flight
Pattern," "Spinning the Bottle," "Bridge," "Magnet"

Harvard Review: "Rhubarb and Garbage"

The Hopkins Review: "Acapulco," "At the Memorial Service,"
    "Nightshirt," "Madrid"

Jewish Currents: "Refusal to Mourn," "Adjacent"

Meetinghouse: "Stretch"

Michigan Quarterly Review: "Daphne"

The New York Review of Books: "Bunker," "Purchase"

The New Yorker: "Conflation," "Springfield"

On the Seawall: "Passing the Torch," "Mantle"

Plume: "Back to School," "Fox," "Piñata"

Quarterly West: "Horses"

Revel: "Materials & Methods"

Terrain: "Stone Age," "Emergency Chocolate Cake," "Sea Shanty,"
    "Freight," "Remember"

The Threepenny Review: "Notes on the Text," "Snake Handler"

Verse Daily: "Eavesdropping on Adam & Eve"

Counterweights to sorrow (*thanks*): Razia Iqbal, Francesca Bewer, Amy Anderson, Giavanna Munafo, Gail Mazur, Robert Pinsky, Andy Senchak, Kiel Moe, Alice Sebold, Tom Sleigh, Sarah Harwell, Ginny Threefoot, Olga Broumas, Jean Wilcox, Bob Steinberg, Lise Motherwell, the Allenbergs, Naomi Wallace, my family, and Bosco. And deep thanks to the Guggenheim Foundation and everyone at Four Way.

Andrea Cohen's poems have appeared in *The New Yorker, The Atlantic Monthly, Poetry, The Threepenny Review, The New York Review of Books*, and elsewhere. Her earlier poetry collections include *Everything, Nightshade, Unfathoming, Furs Not Mine, Kentucky Derby, Long Division*, and *The Cartographer's Vacation*. Awards include a Guggenheim Fellowship and several residencies at MacDowell. She directs the Blacksmith House Poetry Series in Cambridge, MA.

WE ARE ALSO GRATEFUL TO THOSE INDIVIDUALS WHO PARTICIPATED IN
OUR BUILD A BOOK PROGRAM. THEY ARE:

Anonymous (14), Robert Abrams, Michael Ansara, Kathy Aponick,
Michael Anna de Armas, Jean Ball, Sally Ball, Clayre Benzadón,
Adrian Blevins, Laurel Blossom, Adam Bohannon, Betsy Bonner,
Patricia Bottomley, Lee Briccetti, Joel Brouwer, Susan Buttenwieser,
Anthony Cappo, Paul and Brandy Carlson, Dan Clarke, Mark Conway,
Elinor Cramer, Kwame Dawes, John Del Peschio,
Brian Komei Dempster, Patrick Donnelly, Lynn Emanuel,
Blas Falconer, Jennifer Franklin, John Gallaher, Reginald Gibbons,
Rebecca Kaiser Gibson, Dorothy Tapper Goldman, Julia Guez,
Naomi Guttman and Jonathan Mead, Forrest Hamer, Luke Hankins,
Yona Harvey, KT Herr, Karen Hildebrand, Carlie Hoffman,
Glenna Horton, Thomas and Autumn Howard, Catherine Hoyser,
Elizabeth Jackson, Linda Susan Jackson, Jessica Jacobs and
Nickole Brown, Lee Jenkins, Elizabeth Kanell, Nancy Kassell,
Maeve Kinkead, Victoria Korth, Brett Lauer and Gretchen Scott,
Howard Levy, Owen Lewis and Susan Ennis, Margaree Little,
Sara London and Dean Albarelli, Tariq Luthun, Myra Malkin,
Louise Mathias, Victoria McCoy, Lupe Mendez, Michael and
Nancy Murphy, Kimberly Nunes, Susan Okie and Walter Weiss,
Cathy McArthur Palermo, Veronica Patterson, Jill Pearlman,
Marcia and Chris Pelletiere, Sam Perkins, Susan Peters and
Morgan Driscoll, Maya Pindyck, Megan Pinto, Kevin Prufer,
Martha Rhodes and Jean Brunel, Paula Rhodes, Louise Riemer,
Peter and Jill Schireson, Rob Schlegel, Yoana Setzer,
Soraya Shalforoosh, Mary Slechta, Diane Souvaine, Barbara Spark,
Catherine Stearns, Jacob Strautmann, Yerra Sugarman, Arthur Sze
and Carol Moldaw, Marjorie and Lew Tesser, Dorothy Thomas,
Rosalynde Vas Dias, Rushi Vyas, Martha Webster and Robert Fuentes,
Abby Wender and Rohan Weerasinghe, Rachel Weintraub and
Allston James, and Monica Youn.